MW00899074

# Valentine's
## COLORING BOOK
# for Kids

## This Book belongs to:

-------------------------

-------------------------

-------------------------

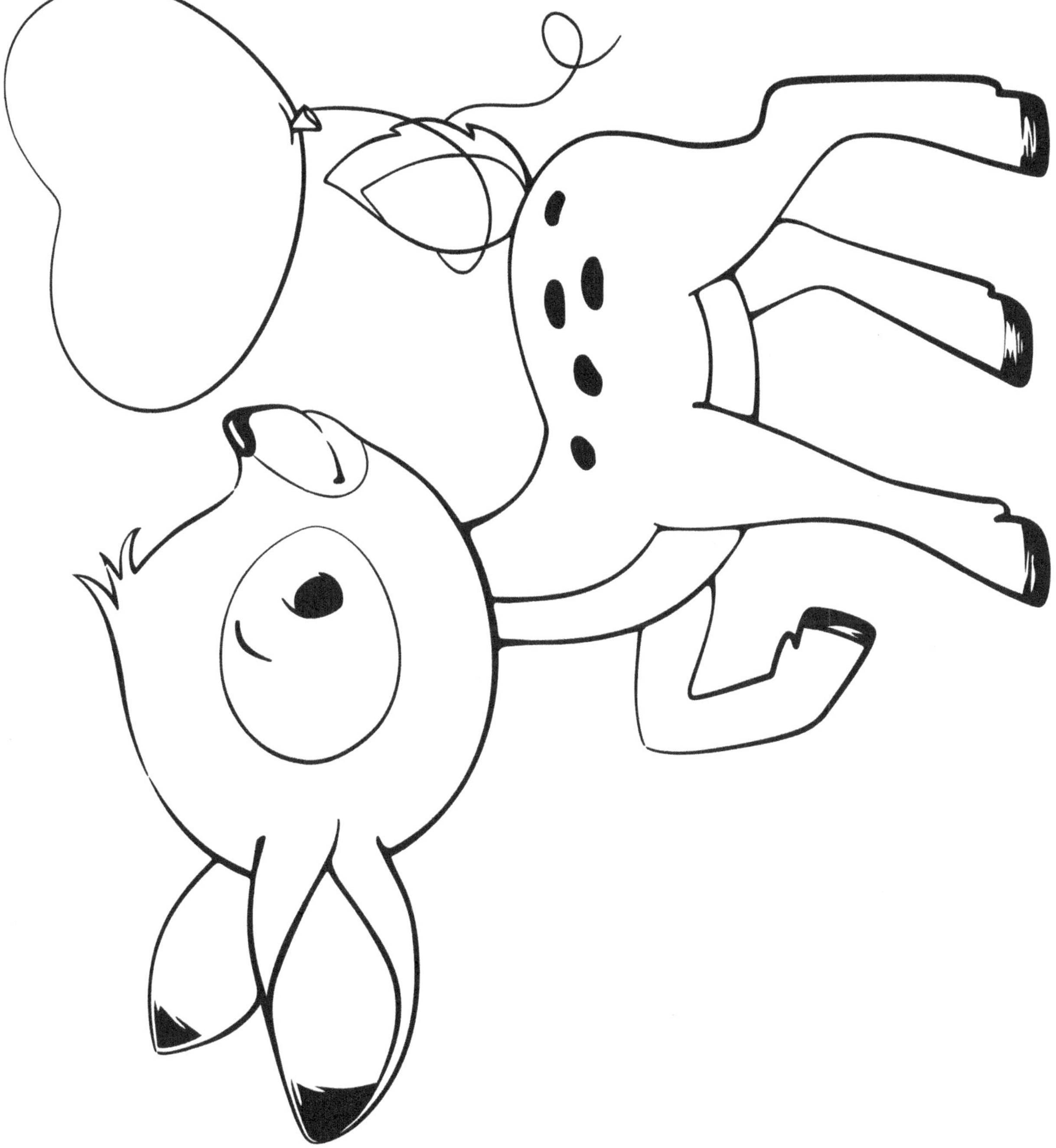

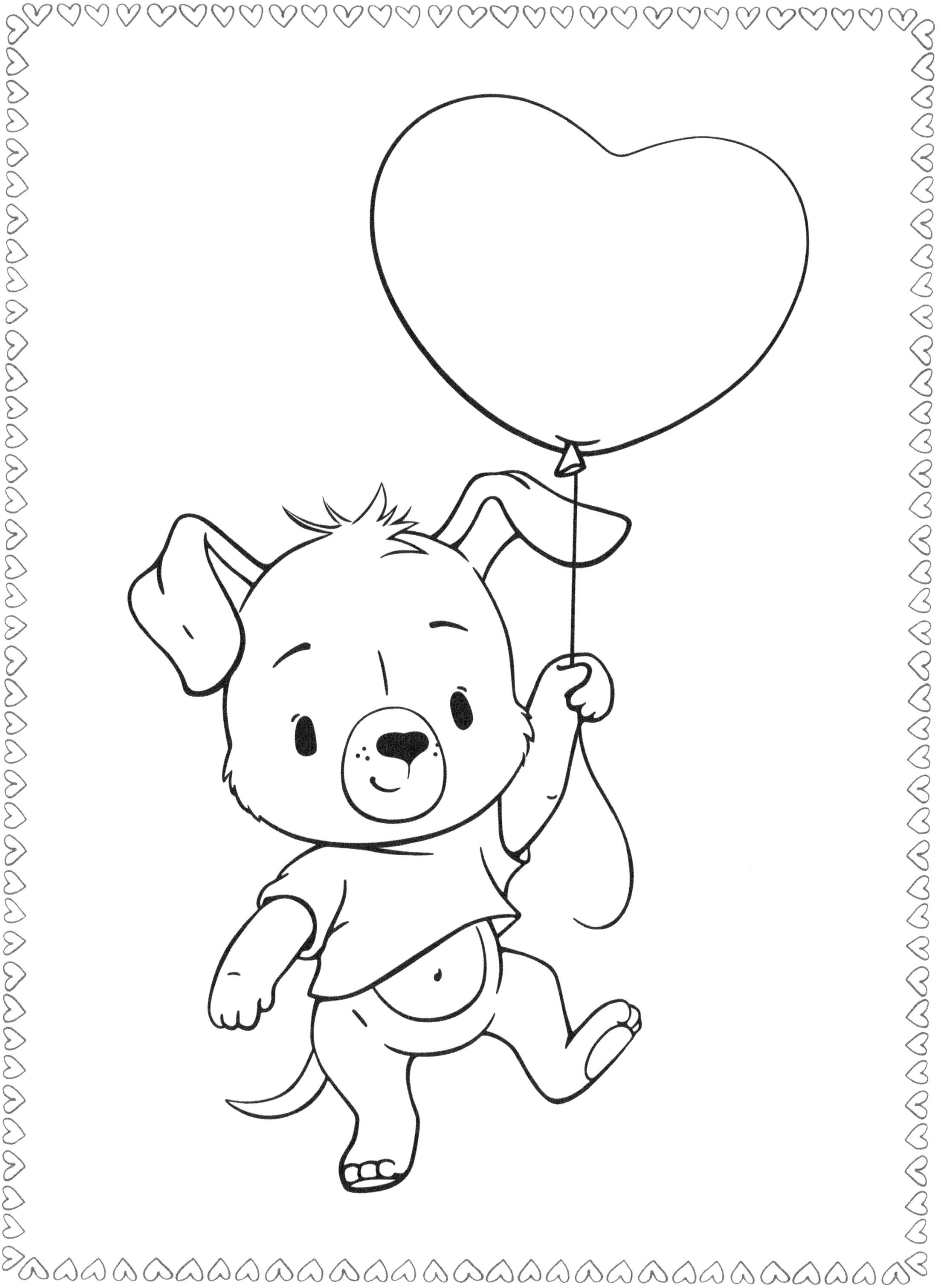

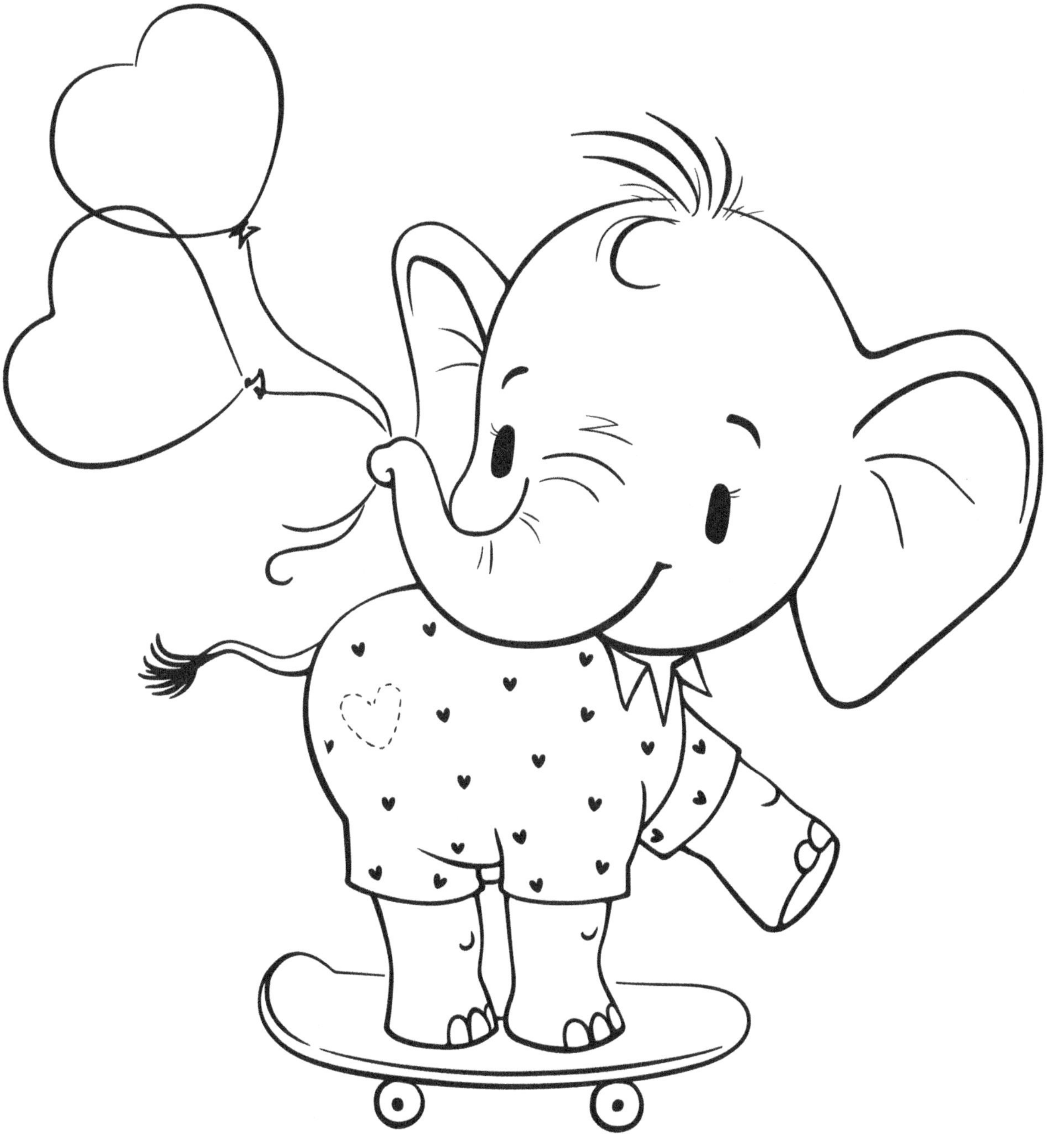

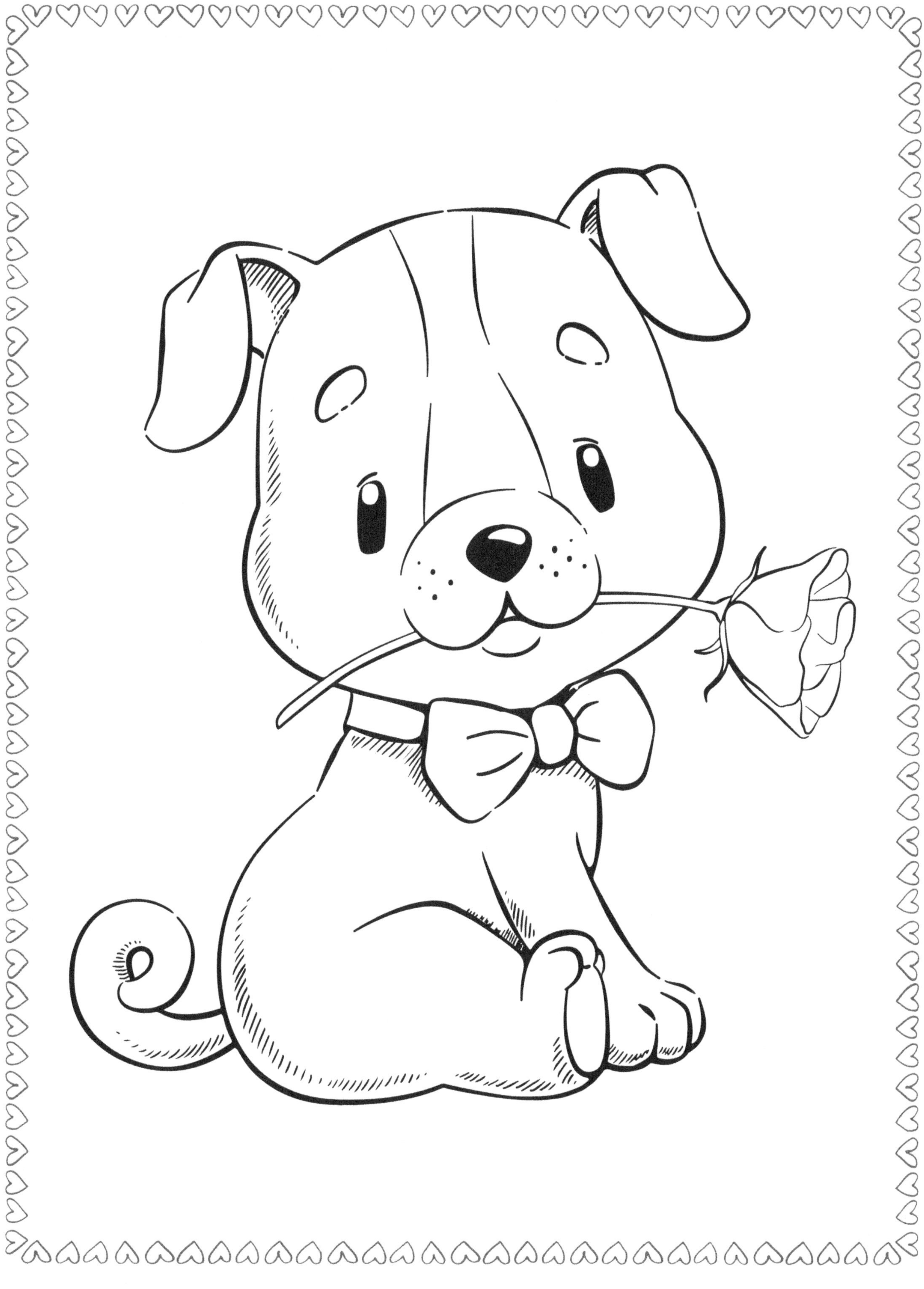

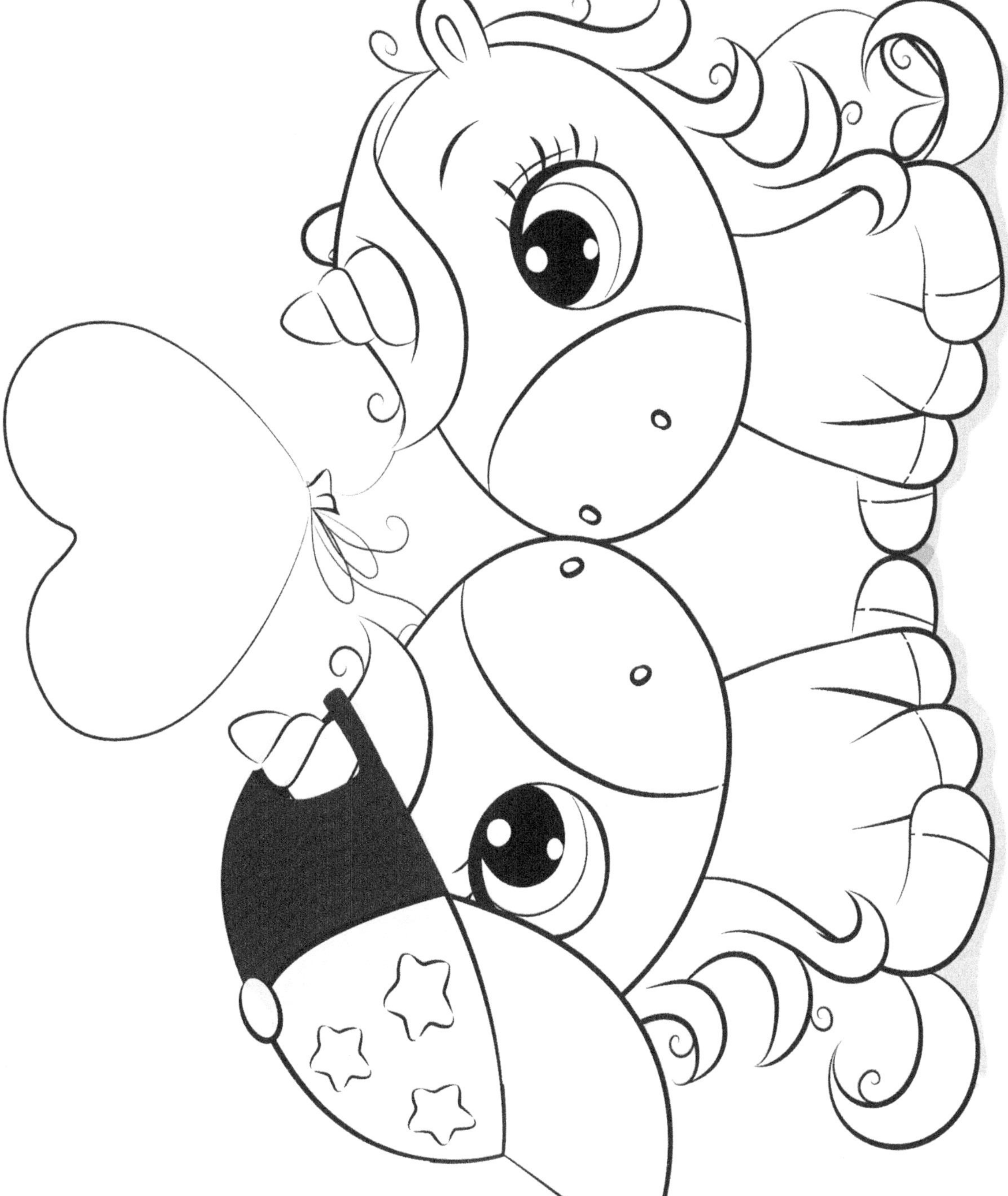

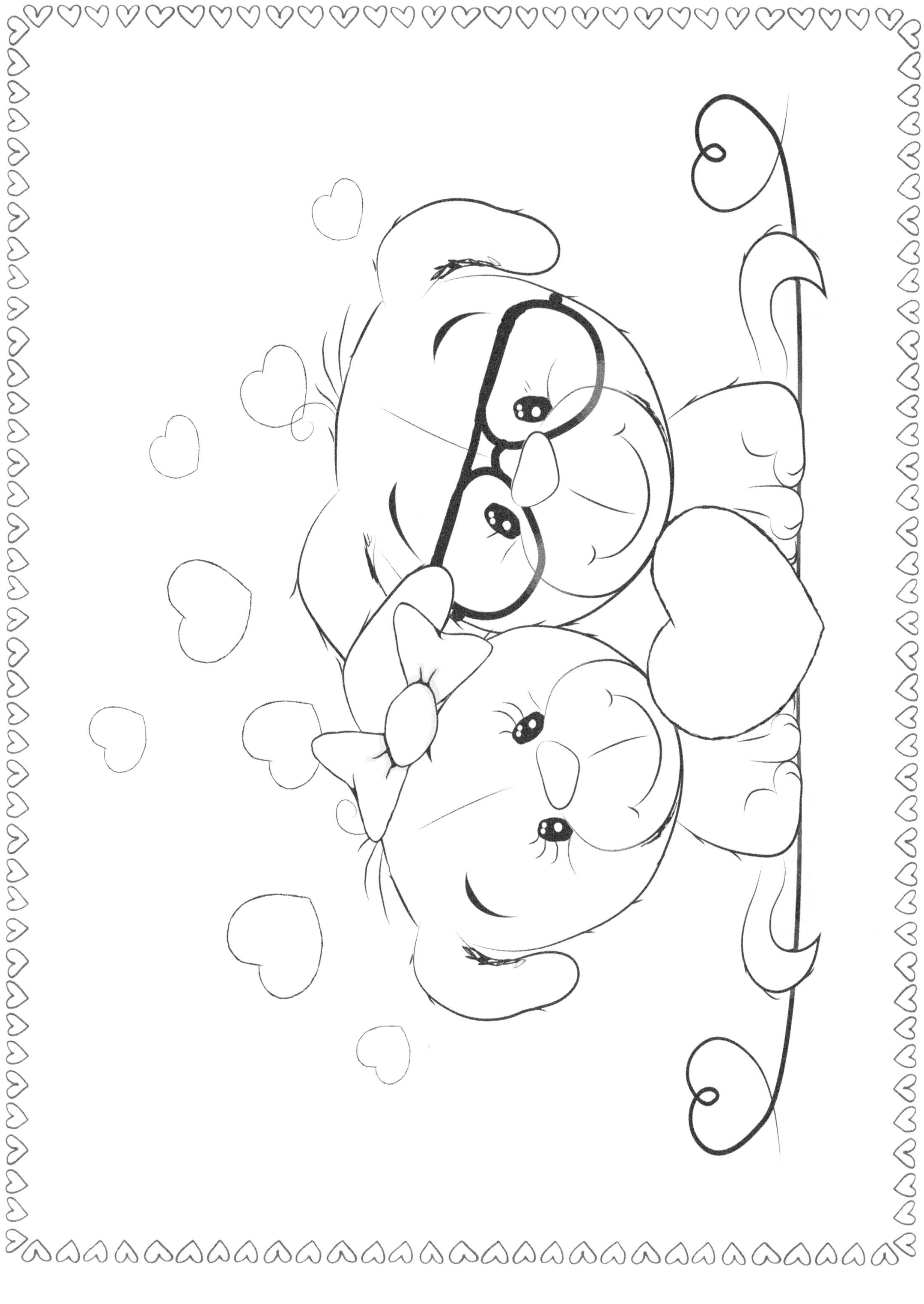

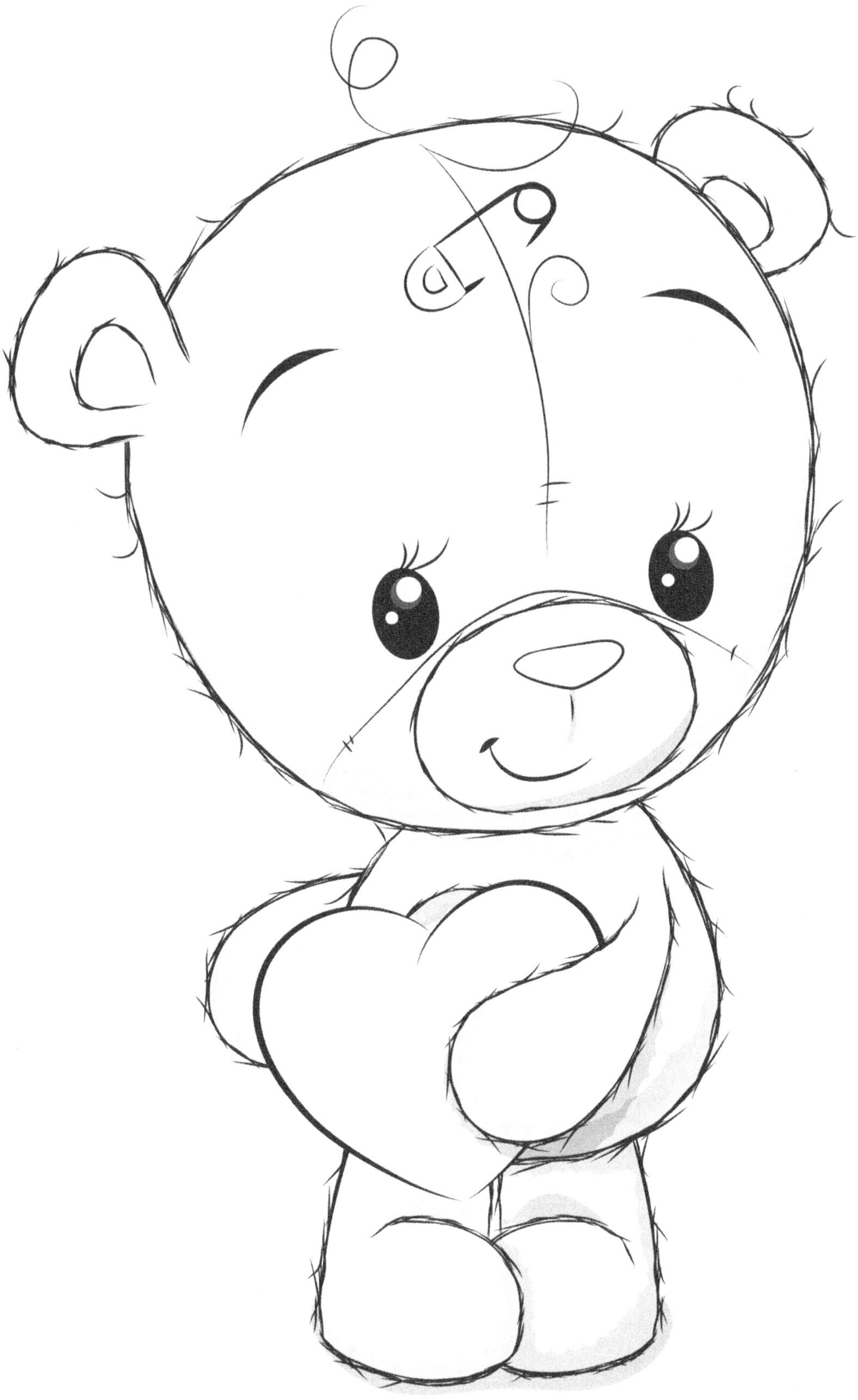

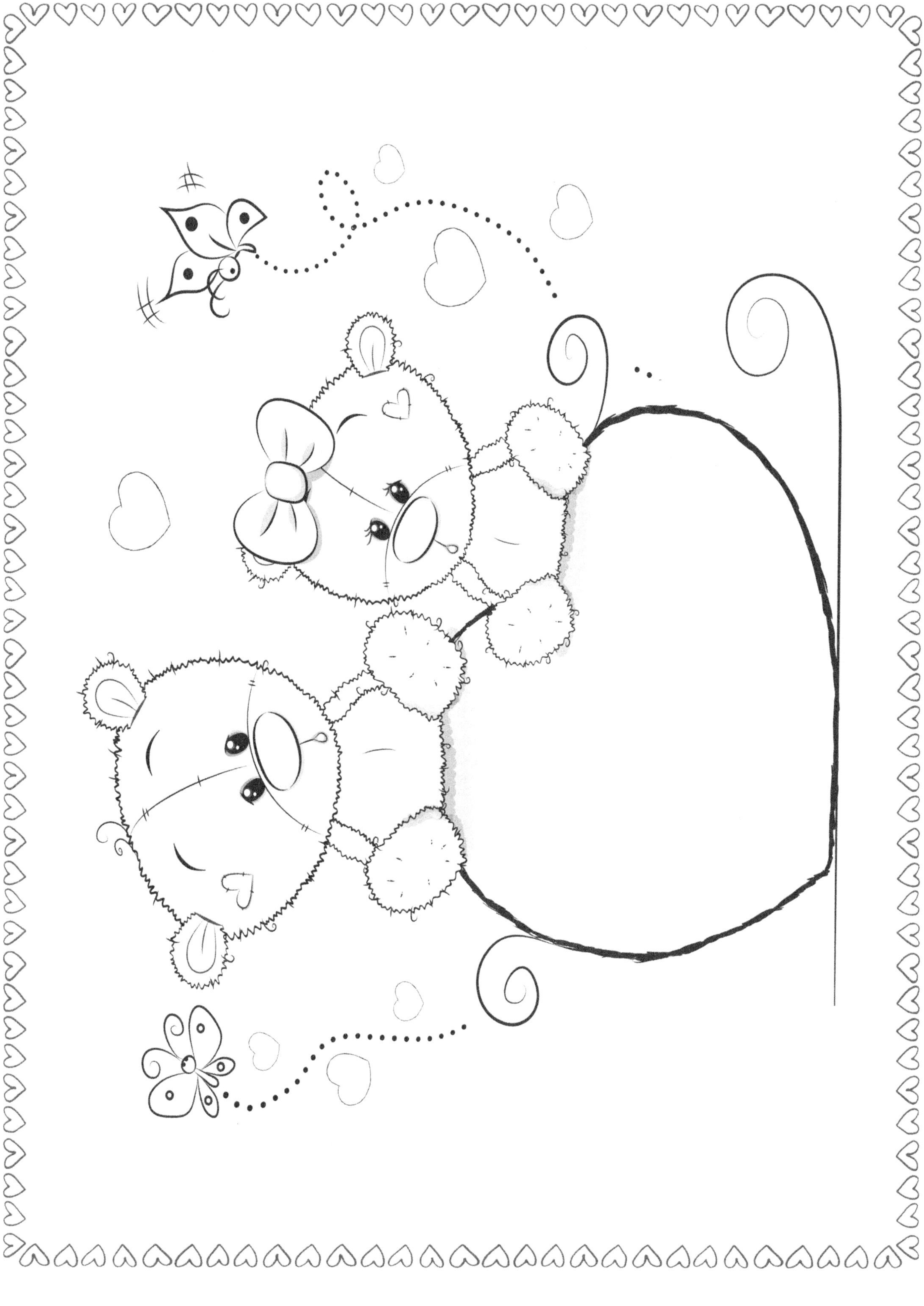

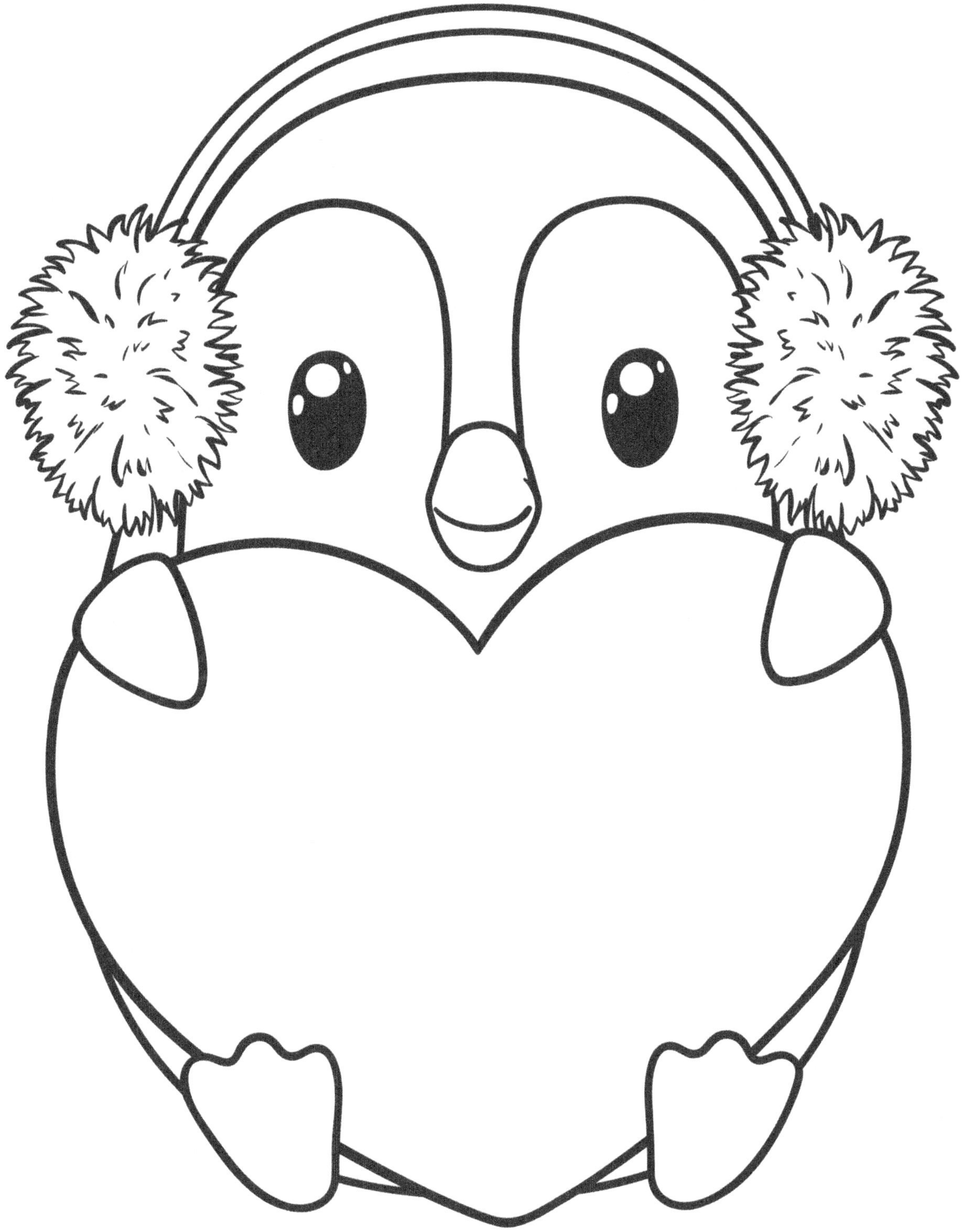

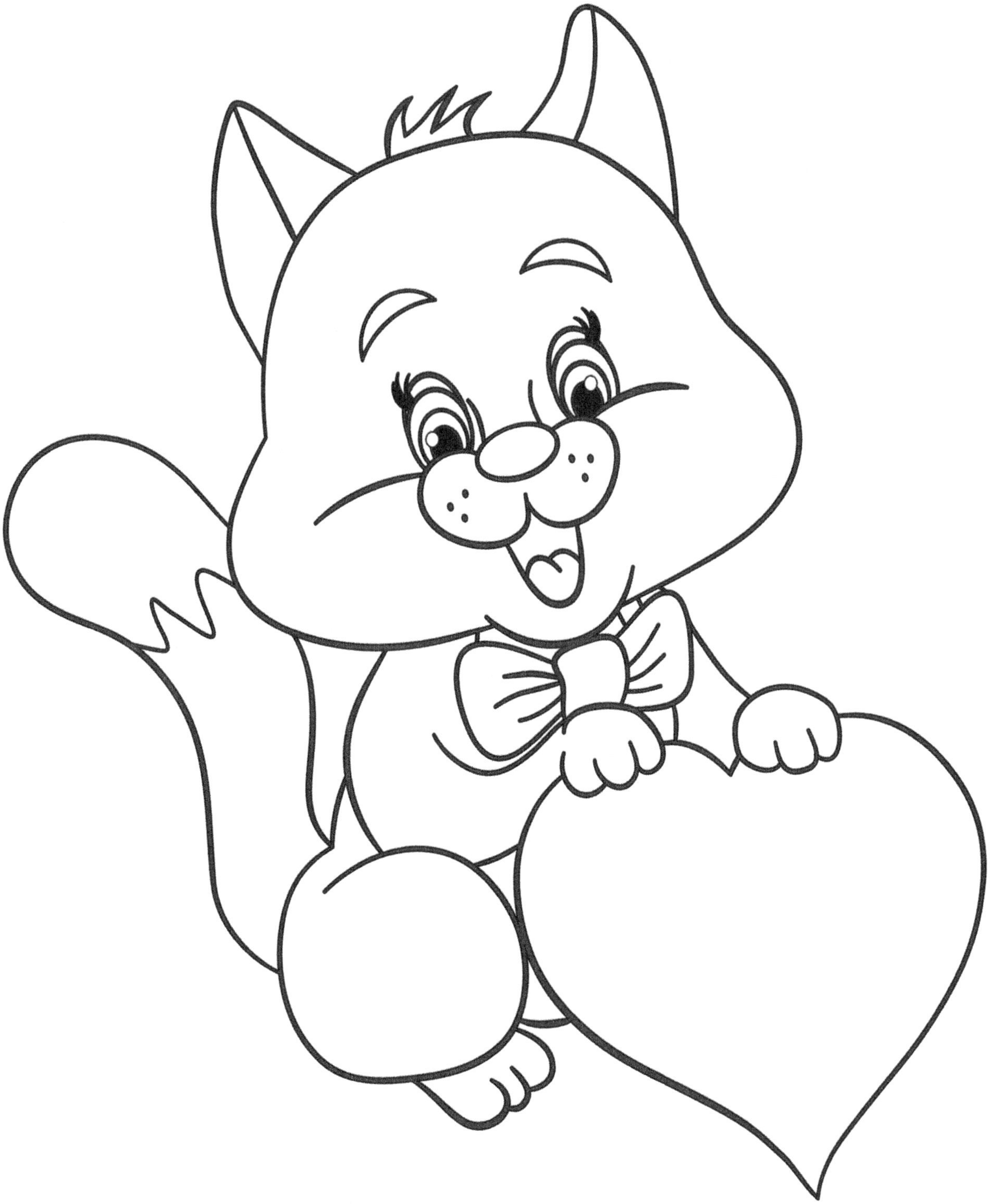

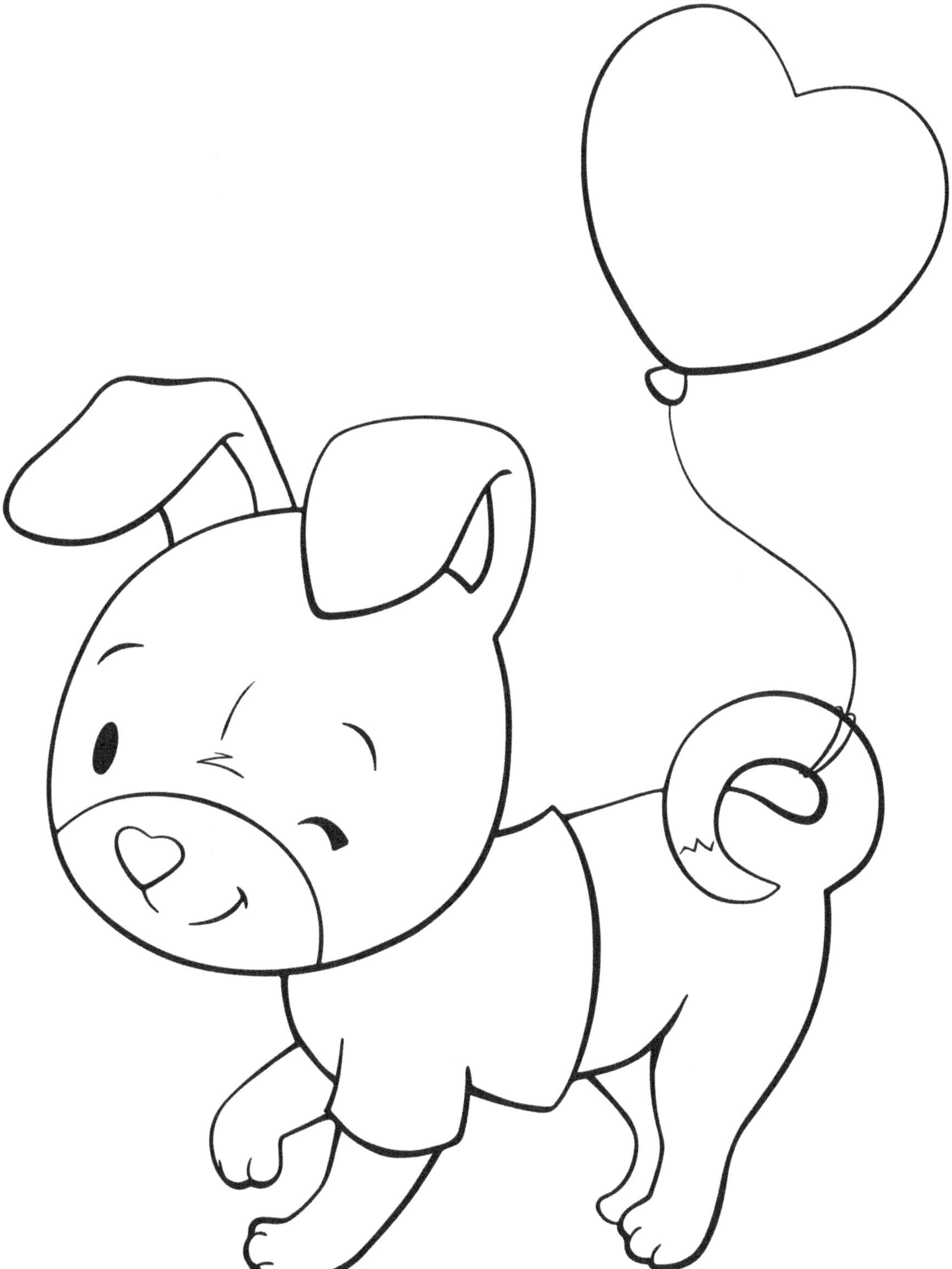

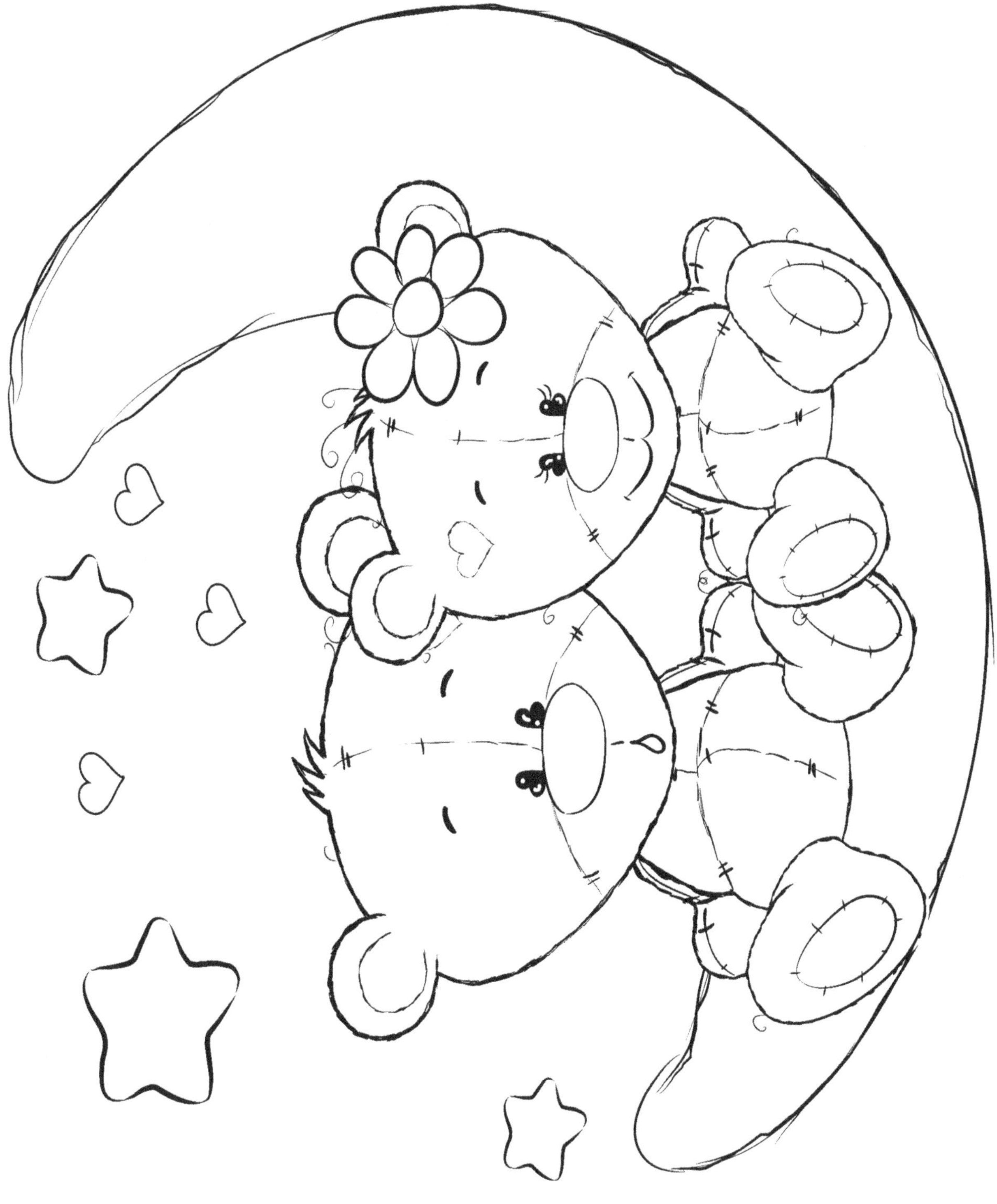

Made in the USA
Coppell, TX
11 February 2020

15716553R00037